The Ethics of Human Development Training Program

-- The Workbook --

David Thomas, PhD

Copyright © 2025, D. Thomas

Copyright © 2025 by David Thomas, PhD

All rights reserved. No part of this publication may be reproduced, stored in a retrieval system, or transmitted, in any form or by any means, electronic, mechanical, photocopying, recording, or otherwise, without the prior written permission of the author.

ISBN: 978-0-578-31400-6

Distributed by Fifty-Six Street Press

Cover art: Paula Ziegman

Cover design: D. Thomas

For more information on *the Ethics of Human Development Training Program*, contact David Thomas, PhD, at dtec@cox.net or go to: davidthomasphd.com.

Introduction[1]

> *NOTE TO THE READER: This workbook is one part of The Ethics of Human Development Training Program. That program consists of several components, principally: Workshop, Workbook, and Evaluation and Feedback System.*
>
> *However, the Workbook can be used on its own. It presents the ethics of human development and it invites a close review of one's relationship with whatever organization is under consideration.*
>
> *Individuals interested in applying the ethics of human development to their work-life will find the Workbook useful, as will organizational personnel and trainers interested in furthering ethical cultures in organizations.*

The purpose of *the Ethics of Human Development Workbook* is to help you identify what you should *know* and *do* to serve both yourself and the various organizations of which you are a part. One of the key assumptions of *The Ethics of Human Development Training Program* is that the ethical path is the path most likely to serve both you and your organization(s) over the long run.

The first point to make concerning your use of this workbook is that it is *for your eyes only*. It is not to be shared with anyone else unless you choose to share it. There are numerous questions in the workbook that ask you to consider sensitive matters. Keeping your answers confidential is important. At the same time, it is important that you answer these questions since it is by addressing these sensitive and real matters that you discern the ethical requirement(s) before you.

The second point is that "the law of intention" governs the extent to which you will find this workbook (and the workshop experience) worthwhile. The law of intention states that with respect to many endeavors in life *we get out equal to what we put in*. The degree to which you take this workbook (and workshop experience) seriously is an important factor determining the degree to which you will benefit from it.

The third point concerns the use of the word "customer". In a sense, we are all one another's customers, all of us, in one way or another, serving and being served. That is the sense in which the term "customer" is being used and for that reason you should not hesitate to substitute whatever specific term more accurately identifies the individuals or group with whom you are involved (i.e., consumers, colleagues, students, clients, fellow employees, family members, etc.)

Fourth, no one lives the totally ethical life. To one degree or another, we all fall short. This workbook (and training program) is built on that assumption, but built also on the assumption that we all can improve, at least by degree.

And who knows what advantages might come to us and to our organizations were we to make even slight improvements?

Finally, while the focus in this workbook (and training program) is on the organization where, in all likelihood, you earn your living, it could focus just as readily on your involvement with other organizations; your family, for example, your circle of friends, the organization where you volunteer your time. The hope is that the training will prove of benefit to all the organizations of which you are a part.

As you begin, remember to proceed thoughtfully and with care. This workbook (and the training program that accompanies it, should you also be taking the training) is designed to serve you and your organizational affiliations in profound and enduring ways. All you must do is give it a full and fair try.

David Thomas, PhD

Purpose of Training Program:

The purpose of *The Ethics of Human Development Training Program is to teach the ethics of human development.* These ethics could be called the ethics of personal growth, the ethics of personal responsibility, the ethics of right livelihood, the ethics of teamwork and collaboration. By whatever name, it is presumed that through our effort to behave ethically, we serve ourselves and others over the long run.

The workbook gives you with the opportunity to examine your relationship to your organization. Hopefully, it will help you identify ways in which you might serve your organization even more effectively.

State Your Intention:

In the space provided, indicate how you intend to approach the questions in this workbook. Just a few words—*truthfully, thoroughly, thoughtfully, etc.*—can help you remember to stay on track as your attention wanes or distractions occur.

_____

_____

_____

_____

Ethic 1: The Organizational Ethic

*It is ethical to
serve, refine, and advance
the organization*
you have chosen to join.
It is unethical to
harm it.*

*For "organization" read: business, corporation, institution,
agency, team, family, etc., as appropriate.

All organizations, whether they are businesses, institutions, or governmental agencies are systems (i.e., networks of mutually influencing parts connected by a common purpose). To harm the system/organization you have chosen to join is, likely, to harm yourself. It is self-destructive. On the other hand, to serve, refine, and advance the organization you have chosen to join is to serve yourself. If the organization is worthy of your involvement, worthy of your contribution, then in all likelihood, as it prospers so do you.

To make this point in terms that are familiar to most of us, it is fair to say that organizations are also teams. To harm your team is to diminish its prospects for success. As its fortunes decline, so do yours. On the other hand, to serve your team, to advance it by developing ways that increase its capacity for success, is to serve yourself. You benefit as your contribution benefits the team. Its successes become yours.

Beyond that, even if the team—despite your contribution—fails to succeed, you benefit because you will have exercised your ability to serve and contribute. This keeps you ready, your muscles exercised should you decide the time has come to join another team.

Thus, it is to your benefit to serve, refine, and advance the organization you have chosen to join. It is to your disadvantage to harm it. From this ethic, several corollaries follow.

> ## Ethic 1: Corollary 1
> *It is ethical to learn everything you can about the organization of which you are a part, including its overall purpose; the vision that guides it; its rules, practices, and procedures; its parts and how they are connected; its history and status.* It is unethical to remain organizationally ignorant.

1) In your own words, state the mission of your organization (this question and the following questions can be answered as well at the level of your department, division, unit, team, etc.):

_____

_____

_____

2) To what extent can you describe the purpose and specific activities of the various divisions, sections and/or units of your organization?

    Completely ___   Considerably ___   Somewhat ___   Not at all ___

3) To what extent has your organization made an effort to educate you (and other members of the organization) to the way in which its parts work as a whole to accomplish the organization's mission?

    Completely ___   Considerably ___   Somewhat ___   Not at all ___

4) To what extent have you, on your own, sought out this knowledge?

    Completely ___   Considerably ___   Somewhat ___   Not at all ___

5) Overall, what would you say are the strengths of your organization or, to put it another way, what do you admire about your organization?

_____

_____

_____

6) What would you say are its weaknesses, those things that concern you about your organization?

_____

_____

_____

7) Overall, how healthy is your organization? (By healthy is meant: capable of serving its mission ethically, creatively, effectively.)

      Extremely ___ Very ___ Somewhat ___ Not at all ___

8) What is the current trend; is it becoming healthier or less healthy?

      Healthier ___ Less Healthy ___ Staying the same ___

9) What are the possible implications or consequences of not learning (and continuing to learn) everything you can about your organization?

    Implications for person who chooses not to learn about the organization?

    _____

    _____

    _____

    Implications for the organization?

    _____

    _____

    _____

Ethic 1: Corollary 2

It is ethical to learn about the needs of those served by your organization (i.e., who they are and what they value), and it is also ethical to learn about the needs of those within the organization served by your division or part. It is unethical to remain ignorant of the needs of those you serve, whether they are customers, consumers, clients, students or fellow employees.

10) What is it that you are trying to provide your customers or, to put it another way, what is it that they value and appreciate about your products or services? What makes them satisfied customers, feeling they have been served well?

_____
_____
_____

11) What about the people with whom you work, your colleagues, co-workers, supervisors, supervisees; what do they count on from you? What makes them satisfied co-workers, feeling they have been served well?

_____
_____
_____

12) What are the possible implications or consequences of remaining ignorant of—and not attending to—the needs of customers and/or fellow workers?

Implications for person who does this?

_____
_____
_____

Implications for the organization?

_____
_____
_____

Ethic 1: Corollary 3

It is ethical to perform your role (i.e., your job or duty) accurately, efficiently, and pleasantly. It is unethical not to do your job to the best of your ability.

13) At what percent of your capacity would you say you are functioning currently?

<u>Enter a number from 5 to 100%:</u>   _____ %

14) How would you rate your performance on the following:

    Accuracy?   Excellent ___ Good ___ Average ___ Poor ___
    Efficiency?   Excellent ___ Good ___ Average ___ Poor ___
    Pleasantness? Excellent ___ Good ___ Average ___ Poor ___

15) If you are not satisfied with your ratings in questions 13 and 14, what is required in order to improve them?

_____

_____

16) What are the possible implications or consequences of not working to the best of your ability?

    Implications for person who does not work to the best of his/her ability?

_____

_____

    Implications for organization or leader who does not call on employees to perform to the best of their ability?

_____

_____

17) For the person who chooses to perform at a consistently high level, what are the possible consequences?

_____

_____

Ethic 1: Corollary 4

It is ethical to perform your role (i.e., your job or duty) in a fashion that does not add to the work, hardship, or distraction of others unnecessarily. It is unethical to make work unnecessarily harder for others.

18) Do you feel that there are people and/or practices in your organization that make your work unnecessarily harder, that add unnecessary hardship or distraction?

                Yes ___ No ___

19) If yes, identify those behaviors and/or organizational practices.

_____

_____

20) How do you feel you score on this issue? Do you think that you ever make work unnecessarily harder for others?

                Yes ___ No ___

21) If so, how? How might you change so as to make things easier on others?

_____

_____

22) What are the implications or consequences of "making work unnecessarily harder for others"?

    Implications for person who does this?

    _____

    _____

    Implications for his or her co-workers?

    _____

    _____

    Implications for organization as a whole?

    _____

    _____

Ethic 1: Corollary 5

It is ethical to speak fairly and honestly of organizational members; to say about them what you are willing to say to them. The same applies to the organization as a whole. It is unethical to engage in malicious gossip, ridicule, or derisive humor.

23) How would you rate your organization on this ethic? To what extent do organizational members speak fairly and honestly, or not at all of others? To what extent do they say about them only what they are willing to say to them?

   Completely ___   Considerably ___   Somewhat ___   Not at all ___

24) Do you ever feel like you are the victim of malicious gossip, ridicule, or derisive humor?

   Yes ___ No ___ Perhaps ___

25) How would you rate yourself on this ethic? To what extent do you speak fairly and honestly of others, saying about them what you are willing to say to them?

   Completely ___   Considerably ___   Somewhat ___   Not at all ___

26) Why do people choose to engage in malicious gossip, ridicule, racist, sexist, or otherwise derisive humor? What do you think are the reasons?

   _____
   _____
   _____

27) What are the implications or consequences of malicious gossip, ridicule, or derisive humor?

   Implications for person who engages in it?

   _____
   _____
   _____

   Implications for the organization?

   _____
   _____
   _____

> ## Ethic 1: Corollary 6
>
> *It is ethical to follow the rules, practices, and procedures of the organization.* It is unethical to willfully and knowingly violate the rules, practices, and procedures of the organization or to remain ignorant of them.
>
> *NOTE: At the same time, it is naive to think that rules are never to be broken. Therefore, it is ethical to make exceptions to rules, practices, and procedures when such exceptions serve or do not harm the organization. Further, it is ethical to share the reasoning behind these exceptions so that this reasoning can be examined and refined and so that others in the organization can sooner recognize when and where exceptions are appropriate. It is ethical to help others in the organization acquire the discernment that allows them to make exceptions to rules, practices, and procedures when such exceptions serve or do not harm the organization.*

28) How would you rate yourself on following the rules, practices, and procedures of your organization?

        Excellent ___ Good ___ Average ___ Poor ___

29) What kind of job would you say your organization has done in helping its members understand the reasoning behind its rules/practices/procedures?

        Excellent ___ Good ___ Average ___ Poor ___

30) To what extent have you, on your own, sought out this knowledge, especially with respect to rules/practices/procedures that strike you as unnecessary, arbitrary, hard to follow?

        Completely ___ Considerably ___ Somewhat ___ Not at all ___

31) What are the implications or consequences of consistently ignoring the rules?

    Implications for person who ignores the rules/practices/procedures?

    _____

    _____

    Implications for this person's supervisor? For the organization?

    _____

    _____

    _____

32) If you are a supervisor, how would you say you do when it comes to requiring adherence to organizational rules, practices, and procedures? When it comes to rules, practices, and procedures that need to be followed, do you require that they be followed or do you look away and avoid the uncomfortable task of holding people accountable? How would you rate yourself when it comes to upholding the rules, practices, and procedures of your organization?

Excellent ___ Good ___ Average ___ Poor ___

33) Here are four rules or practices common to many organizations. Rate yourself on your adherence to these items and then, if you are a supervisor, rate how well you hold your supervisees to these rules and practices.

You don't have to rate yourself on paper. Instead, rate yourself privately, in your own mind, from 10 -- "excellent" to 1 -- "needs a lot of improvement". First, rate your own performance and then, if a supervisor, rate your willingness to hold the line with others. Be honest with yourself.

- not abusing sick leave
- not using the organization's property or supplies for one's own purposes
- not padding travel or personal reimbursement requests
- not divulging confidential information

34) What are the implications or consequences of violating the rules concerning one or more of the four items just considered?

Implications for person who violates the rules?

_____
_____

Implications for the person's supervisor?

_____
_____

Implications for the organization?

_____
_____
_____

Ethic 1: Corollary 7

It is ethical to seek the correction, modification, and/or revision of rules, practices, and procedures that are inconsistent with the overall purpose and stated values of the organization. It is unethical to accept without seeking to correct organizational practices that harm the ability of the organization to accomplish its purpose.

35) Do you think that there are rules, practices, or procedures currently in place in your organization that are inconsistent with its purpose and stated values?

Yes ___ No ___

36) If yes, what are they and in what way do they harm the ability of the organization to accomplish its purpose?

_____
_____
_____
_____
_____
_____

37) Have you made an effort to correct these problems?   Yes ___ No ___

38) If yes, what have you done?

_____
_____
_____

39) If not, or if unsuccessful so far, what might you do, if anything, to correct these problems?

_____
_____
_____

> # Ethic 1: Corollary 8
>
> *It is ethical to create organizational improvements. These improvements may be in the form of or result in increased revenue, decreased costs, improved services, or an enhanced organizational culture.* But whatever the form or result, it is unethical not to help the organization evolve.

40) How would you rate yourself on this ethic? Do you feel as though you have made an improvement (no matter how small) that in some way has helped the organization grow, develop, become more effective?

Yes ___ No ___

41) From your point of view, what improvements (large or small) are needed in your part of the organization?

_____
_____
_____

42) Which of these, if any, do you believe you could do something about?

_____
_____
_____

43) In general terms, what could you do?

_____
_____
_____

44) In what way does your proposed improvement benefit the organization?

       ___ increased revenue
       ___ decreased costs
       ___ improved services
       ___ improved workplace culture
       ___ other: _____

45) What would be the costs to the organization to implement your improvement? And what would be the benefits? How would you measure both?

_____
_____
_____

46) What role are you willing and able to play in the creation of your proposed improvement (i.e., footwork, research, cost/benefit analysis, politics, creating a team, etc.)?

_____
_____
_____

47) Can you accomplish your proposed improvement without interfering with your other duties?

Yes ___ No ___

48) Is there any part of your proposed improvement that infringes on what others would perceive as their "turf"? If so, how would you approach these individuals so as to enlist their support?

_____
_____
_____

49) What are the implications or consequences of attempting to create improvements and thus, bring about improvements in the organization?

Implications for person who does this?

_____
_____

Implications for this person's supervisor? Fellow employees?

_____
_____

Implications for the organization?

_____
_____

Ethic 1: Corollary 9

It is ethical to protect and defend the organization against destructive influences such as outside forces or internal decision-making practices that lead to fraud, libel, or abuse. It is unethical to remain silent in the face of perceived threats to the organization's survival.

50) Do you believe that your organization is currently threatened by either outside forces or its own internal practices?

       Yes ___ No ___

51) If yes, what are they?

_____
_____
_____

52) If these threats are not known about generally, have you done your part to make the appropriate parties aware of them?

       Yes ___ No ___

53) In your view, is your organization currently taking adequate steps to meet the threat?

       Yes ___ No ___

54) If not, what would you suggest it do?

_____
_____
_____

55) Have you offered this suggestion to the appropriate parties? Yes ___ No ___

56) If not, why not?

_____
_____
_____

> # Ethic 1: Corollary 10
>
> *It is ethical to leave an organization whose purpose and values conflict with your own.* It is unethical to remain in an organization that requires you to violate your values or personal code of ethics.

57) Circle the level of importance to you of each of the values listed below.

	How important is this value to you?				
	Not at all				Extremely
Compassion	1	2	3	4	5
Courage	1	2	3	4	5
Courtesy	1	2	3	4	5
Creativity	1	2	3	4	5
Effectiveness	1	2	3	4	5
Fairness	1	2	3	4	5
Flexibility	1	2	3	4	5
Humility	1	2	3	4	5
Kindness	1	2	3	4	5
Orderliness	1	2	3	4	5
Openness	1	2	3	4	5
Personal relationships	1	2	3	4	5
Supportiveness	1	2	3	4	5
Sustainability	1	2	3	4	5
Wellbeing	1	2	3	4	5

Others: _____   1 2 3 4 5

_____   1 2 3 4 5

58) While there will be differences between you and your organization on the values listed, are there, in your judgment, serious points of conflict?

Yes ___ No ___

59) If yes, what are they?

_____

_____

60) Given the purpose and values of your organization, are you and your organization a good fit?

                        Yes ___ No ___

61) If not, do you feel as though you can bring about a change either in the organization or yourself, or both that will allow you to serve your organization wholeheartedly?

                        Yes ___ No ___

62) If yes, what do you plan to do? What is the change you have in mind and how will you bring it about?

_____

_____

_____

63) If such a change is not possible and you believe you no longer can be a member of your organization, how can you leave responsibly? What steps can you take to ensure that both your needs and, hopefully, the organization's needs as well are honored as you go your separate ways?

_____

_____

_____

_____

_____

64) What are the implications or consequences of remaining in an organization whose purpose and values conflict with your own?

    Implications for person who does this?

_____

_____

_____

Implications for this person's family?

_____
_____
_____

Implications for the organization?

_____
_____
_____

Go to the *One Week Action Plan* located at the end of the workbook (p. 79). Read the instructions and answer the three questions on the Organizational Ethic.

This page is reserved for notes and reflections, also for questions and exercises used in the Workshop.

Ethic 2 - The Open Mindedness Ethic[2]

It is ethical to be open to the possibility that your view is incomplete, capable of expansion and improvement. It is unethical to ignore information that could allow you or your organization to grow.

The organization of which you are a part (i.e., its component parts, the personalities of its members, its many connections with the larger community) is enormously complex. Any one person's view within such complexity is necessarily incomplete. It is ethical, therefore, to be open to information that might lead to a more complete view. Absolute certainty, as ethicist John David Garcia writes, is an illusion.[3] It is stultifying, whereas openness to new and relevant information can bring revision, advantage, and growth.

Further, to presume that your view is complete is to announce to others that you have nothing else to learn, that no new information could be received that would lead you to revise your view. This discourages input and eventually, creativity. Openness, on the other hand, makes it possible for both you and your organization to learn, revise, and create.[4]

Ethic 2: Corollary 1

When seeking a more complete formulation or a difficult-to-find solution, it is helpful to ask others what they think. But it is also helpful to precede your own statements of presumed fact with phrases that leave open the possibility that you may not be right. For example, phrases like: "As I see it now," "I may be wrong, but it looks to me as if," or "My experience in these matters leads me to conclude . . . ") support creative discourse. Such phrases qualify the finality of whatever follows and leave room for creative problem solving. It is unethical to speak to deny creative input from others.

65) How would you rate your organization on this ethic and this corollary? To what extent does the interaction style at your organization invite creative input from its members?

    Completely ___ Considerably ___ Somewhat ___ Not at all ___

66) How would you rate yourself on this ethic? To what extent does your interaction style invite creative input from others?

    Completely ___ Considerably ___ Somewhat ___ Not at all ___

67) To what extent do you have the confidence to not always be right, to leave open the possibility that you may be wrong?

    Completely ___ Considerably ___ Somewhat ___ Not at all ___

68) When you are debating an issue with someone who is totally certain of their position, certain beyond all doubt, what is the affect on you? How do you find yourself coping with such a person? Do you "shut down," walk away, argue, feel yourself diminished, get angry? What are your feelings when in such an interaction?

    _____
    _____

69) What do you think is the impact on an organization when its members fail to remain open or when they fail to invite input? What are the implications of this attitude for the organization?

    _____
    _____

> ## Ethic 2: Corollary 2
>
> *It is ethical to be open to the possibility that you yourself, or some unknown factor, may be responsible—however minutely—for the undesirable events or outcomes that come your way.* It is unethical to presume absolute certainty concerning the failure or fault of others. Such absolute certainty can obscure or cut short the examination of other factors and lead to destructive action against individuals rather than to one's growth as a person or to improvements that benefit the organization.

70) To what extent would you say the members of your organization participate in the "blame game," seeking to affix blame rather than focusing on solutions?

    Completely ___ Considerably ___ Somewhat ___ Not at all ___

71) What about you? To what extent do you participate in the "blame game," determining the blame of others rather than pursuing solutions?

    Completely ___ Considerably ___ Somewhat ___ Not at all ___

72) To what extent would you say you are an "open" person, open-minded, inviting of input, capable of being wrong without being threatened, ready to share your thoughts and ideas on issues?

    Completely ___ Considerably ___ Somewhat ___ Not at all ___

73) In your view, what contributes to openness within an organization?

_____
_____
_____

74) How would you score yourself on the factors you've just identified?

    Excellent ___ Good ___ Average ___ Poor ___

75) Of the factors you've identified, which do you most need to work on in order to increase your openness? How can you work on it?

_____
_____
_____

Ethic 3 - The Deliberate Action Ethic

It is ethical to choose consciously and execute deliberately specific actions that you believe represent the best of your discernible options. When the time to act has come, it is unethical not to do something.[5]

(Ethic 3 is the companion ethic to Ethic 2; each without the other is incomplete.)

Though absolute certainty is unavailable (Ethic 2), individuals nevertheless must act. And their actions are most likely to be of value (to themselves if not to others) if they are consciously selected and deliberately executed. Only in this way can individuals test *and strengthen* the adequacy of their decision-making.

Deliberate acts are like experiments. Through them the adequacy of the decision-maker's hypothesis is tested. The feedback that results from these "experiments" (see Ethic 4) allows the decision-maker to learn, to gain confidence, and, if necessary, to correct his or her course of action.

Little or nothing, however, is learned from inaction and much harm can result from it. John David Garcia, scientist and philosopher, has pointed out that "creativity is destroyed by inaction," and adds that each of us will "fail in our [ethical] purpose if (when the time to act has come) we take no action."[6] From the organization's point of view, inaction is unethical because it results in drift, and drift leads only to problems the organization could have avoided had its decision-makers acted when the time to act arrived.

> ## Re-statement of Ethic 3
>
> *When choice points arrive, it is ethical to consciously choose and deliberately execute the best of your discernable options. When the time to act has come, it is unethical not to do something.*

76) What percent of your time at work would you say is spent "on top of it", i.e., conscious, deliberate, purposeful, and what percent would you say is governed by habit, drift, "just going along," "phoning in performance," i.e., unconscious?

      Conscious & Deliberate _____% plus Drifting _____% = 100%

77) Within your organization, are there areas of your performance or responsibility that you have allowed to become habit-governed but which now should be re-thought and your performance perhaps changed?

                  Yes ___   No ___

78) If yes, what are they?

    _____

    _____

    _____

79) Do you procrastinate when the time to act has come?

        Always ___   Often ___   Sometimes ___   Never ___

80) When you see that the time has come to act on an issue important to you and/or the organization but uncomfortable for you to face, how long do you wait to act?

        Not at all ___   1 day ___   up to 1 week ___   longer ___

81) Why is it unethical not to do something when faced with issues important to you or the organization? To put it another way, why is it important to act when you know that the time to act has come?

    _____

    _____

    _____

82) List below your duties and/or general areas of organizational responsibility and rate the degree to which you proceed consciously and deliberately in each area, the degree to which you are "on top of it."

(Scale: 1= Not at all to 5 = Completely)

Areas of responsibility or job duties: Rating:

_____   _____

_____   _____

_____   _____

_____   _____

_____   _____

_____   _____

_____   _____

83) In reviewing your ratings to questions 82, which of your duties or areas of responsibility is most in need of your attention?

_____

_____

_____

84) What in your judgment is the first step you need to take with respect to the area identified in question 83?

_____

_____

_____

Go to the *One Week Action Plan* located at the end of the workbook (p. 80). Answer the Open-Mindedness Ethic and the Deliberate Action Ethic questions.

Ethic 4 - The Feedback Ethic

It is ethical to request, encourage, and deliver feedback. It is unethical to ignore or discourage feedback.

Feedback (and the evaluation of performance implicit in it) is the way in which individuals and organizations become conscious of themselves. Without feedback, learning—except in its most rudimentary form—cannot occur. Thus, feedback offers individuals and organizations course-correcting information, information vital to their effectiveness, vital to their effort to accomplish their purpose.

If feedback is discouraged or ignored, then drift and waste are likely to occur. The responsiveness of the organization diminishes. Its ability to detect and then respond to problems and opportunities decreases threatening, perhaps, the organization's survival. Thus, it is unethical and irresponsible to ignore or discourage feedback.

NOTE: This is not to say that you act on every bit of feedback that you receive, only that you do not ignore or discourage feedback.

At the same time, it is important to remember that the feedback we give others reveals (potentially) as much about us, and what we value, as it does about the performance of the individuals to whom we are giving the feedback. For that reason, we must give feedback sensitively and receive it graciously, realizing that the feedback we give may be wrong and the feedback we receive may be correct.[7]

> # Ethic 4: Corollary 1
>
> *It is ethical to request and encourage feedback on your performance, product(s), and materials from individuals with whom you interact and/or who, in one way or another, receive your services whether they are inside or outside the organization.* It is unethical to ignore or discourage feedback.

85) How would you rate yourself on this corollary? Are you open to feedback? Do you invite it, welcome it, request it? How would you rate yourself?

        Excellent ___ Good ___ Average ___ Poor ___

86) How would your supervisor and those you work with rate you on this corollary? Would they say you are open to and welcoming of feedback? How would they rate you?

        Excellent ___ Good ___ Average ___ Poor ___

87) How would your family—your spouse or significant-other or children or parents—rate you on this corollary?

        Excellent ___ Good ___ Average ___ Poor ___

88) Select and write in the space provided the name of a specific customer or customer group (i.e., consumers, clients, students, co-workers, family, etc.) from whom it would be helpful to receive feedback concerning your interpersonal manner, your performance, product(s) or services.

        Customer(s): _____

89) On what would you like this customer or customer group to provide feedback (performance, quality of service, specific products, materials, etc.)?

_____

_____

_____

_____

> # Ethic 4: Corollary 2
>
> *It is ethical to offer feedback to those from whom you or your organization receive services.* It is ethical to acknowledge outstanding performance, just as it is ethical to provide feedback to those whose performance or service threatens the optimal performance of you or your organization. In both cases, it may be unethical not to do so.

90) How would you rate yourself on this corollary? Are you good about acknowledging—in whatever way is appropriate for you—outstanding performance?

       Excellent ___ Good ___ Average ___ Poor ___

91) How about when it comes to giving feedback to someone whose performance is hurting your performance, or the performance of the organization or team? Do you provide feedback in such a circumstance or do you let it go by? How would you rate yourself?

       Excellent ___ Good ___ Average ___ Poor ___

92) How would others in the organization (supervisor, co-workers, supervisees) rate you on this corollary? Would they say you acknowledge outstanding performance and that you give, as needed, critical and corrective feedback? How would they rate you?

       Excellent ___ Good ___ Average ___ Poor ___

93) Is there an individual or group that provides you, your workgroup, or your organization with particularly outstanding service? If so, who? How might you acknowledge that performance?

_____

_____

94) Is there an individual or group that provides you, your workgroup, or your organization with less than satisfactory service, either in the nature of the service itself or in the way it is provided? If so, who? How might you let them know of your concern? What *constructive* feedback could you offer?

_____

_____

_____

> # Ethic 4: Corollary 3
>
> *It is ethical to deliver feedback sensitively/clearly/directly and to accept it graciously.* It is unethical to diminish the person to whom you are giving feedback or to punish the person from whom you are receiving it.

95) How would you rate yourself on this corollary? It is one thing to request feedback and to deliver it, but when it is offered do you receive it graciously? When you give feedback do you give it sensitively/clearly/directly? How would you rate yourself on this corollary?

      Excellent ___ Good ___ Average ___ Poor ___

96) How would others in the organization (supervisor, co-workers, supervisees, perhaps even family or friends) rate you on this corollary?

      Excellent ___ Good ___ Average ___ Poor ___

97) Think back to the most recent incident in which someone offered you feedback.

For the purposes of this exercise, it need not be feedback from someone in your organization. It can be feedback from a friend, a neighbor, a family member. How did you respond? Indicate the topic on which you were provided feedback. Indicate whether or not the feedback was given in a reasonable manner. And finally, indicate how you responded.

When rating your response, use the following scale (more than one rating possible):

        1 = defensive &/or attacking
        2 = resentful &/or tuning out
        3 = resignation &/or hurt
        4 = considering/accepting as best you can

Topic (abbreviate):	Reasonable approach? (y/n)	Rate your response:
_____	_____	_____

98) Regardless of whether or not the feedback referred to in question 97 was given thoughtfully or in a reasonable manner, was there merit to the content of the feedback? Thinking about the content objectively, was the feedback about something that in your view you should change or do differently?

Yes ___ No ___

99) If so, have you acted on the feedback, initiating the change that is called for?

Yes ___ If not, what might you do?

_____

_____

_____

100) Think back to the most recent incident in which you gave someone corrective or critical feedback.

Again, for the purposes of this exercise, it need not involve someone in your organization but instead can involve a friend, a neighbor, a family member. Indicate the topic on which you provided feedback. Rate the way in which you think you delivered the feedback. And finally, indicate whether or not the desired change occurred.

When rating your delivery, use the following scale:

1 = delivered with anger or resentment
2 = delivered with sarcasm
3 = delivered with indifference
4 = delivered thoughtfully/sensitivity/clearly/directly

Topic (abbreviate):	Rating of delivery:	Desired result?
_____	_____	_____

101) With respect to the episode just discussed, is there anything you would do differently were you to do it again? If so, what?

_____

_____

_____

Ethic 5 - The Truth-Telling Ethic

It is ethical to tell the truth, to be honest. It is unethical to lie. Lying creates misinformation, confusion, and distrust.

Truth-telling (i.e., honesty) builds trust. Trust allows people to relax, to drop their guard, and to level with one another. Truth-telling invites truth-telling. An organization characterized by truth-telling is free of denial and is more likely to deal with issues as they arise. Its capacity to respond with both corrective and creative action increases as there is less confusion in the organization.

It is unethical to lie. As Garcia points out, lying puts misinformation in an organization.[8] Misinformation undermines trust and increases the wariness and confusion of the organization's members. In this way the organization's reaction time to both problems and opportunities decreases.

That is not to say, however, that there are not times when the answer to a question is none of the questioner's business. Or times when expressing the truth as you see it serves only to hurt others. At such times it is truthful and ethical to say, for example, that for personal reasons, or for the sake of your privacy or someone else's, you do not discuss such matters.

Here, as elsewhere with the ethics of human development, there are exceptions. Obviously, if by telling the truth we put someone's life in danger or hurt their feelings unnecessarily, we make an exception. But making exceptions is a tricky business. Exceptions should not be made for personal gain or convenience. Only if the individual cannot utilize the truth for personal growth are we justified in withholding it. And making such a judgment requires a discernment of such an exalted degree that only "genuine love for the other" can drive it. This was M. Scott Peck's point in his book, *The Road Less Traveled*, and having made this point he cautions, *"...in assessing the capacity of another to utilize the truth for personal/spiritual growth, it should be borne in mind that our tendency is generally to underestimate rather than overestimate this capacity."*[9]

> ## Restatement of Ethic 5
>
> *It is ethical to tell the truth, to be honest. Truth-telling promotes clarity and allows you to match resources with greater precision to the demands of the moment.* It is unethical to lie. Lying creates misinformation, confusion, and distrust, threatening your ability (and the organization's ability) to survive, adapt, and prosper.

102) How would you rate your organization on this ethic? Is it characterized by truth-telling, by openness and honesty in matters affecting you and others?

        Excellent ___ Good ___ Average ___ Poor ___

103) How would you rate yourself on this ethic? Do you, at work, for example, trust yourself to tell the truth when representing your view, your performance. (Note: Telling the truth means calmly and thoughtfully telling your truth, not lying for the sake of convenience, fear, or gain.)

        Excellent ___ Good ___ Average ___ Poor ___

104) Are there specific individuals in the organization—individuals in positions of authority, for example—with whom you have a difficult time sharing your truth when your view differs from theirs? If so, what are the reasons? the fears?

_____

_____

_____

105) Sometimes individuals feel they can't share their truth because they feel they lack the skill or tact to express it. They're afraid they will appear harsh or insensitive. Do you ever stop yourself from telling your truth for this reason?

        Yes ___ No ___

If so, how would you describe the skill that you need in order to express yourself:

_____

_____

_____

106) Sometimes individuals feel they can't share their truth because they might hurt

other people's feelings if they do. They remain silent or say what they think the other person wants to hear rather than expressing the truth of their view (or the truth of their feelings). Do you ever stop yourself from telling your truth, your view, for this reason when, in fact, you know you should?

Yes ___ No ___

If so, are you ever mad at yourself as a consequence? What are you losing by not expressing your truth, your view? No one should hurt the feelings of others unnecessarily but when you feel you are in a situation in which you should tell your truth and you stop yourself, what is the cost to you and the other person(s)?

_____

_____

_____

107) According to many serious thinkers and philosophers, one of the most important steps an individual can take in his or her life is to make a commitment to honesty, and to do so completely, with self, family, friends, organizational members, etc. If "100" reflects a total commitment and "0" represents no commitment at all, what score would you give yourself?

_____

108) What are the benefits resulting from conduct in accord with this ethic?

    Benefits for person who adheres to this ethic?

_____

_____

_____

    Benefits for the organization when individuals adhere to this ethic?

_____

_____

_____

Go to the One Week Action Plan located at the end of the workbook (p. 80-81).
Answer the Feedback Ethic and the Truth-Telling Ethic questions.

Ethic 6 - The Pain-Directed Ethic

It is ethical to work first on the issue causing the organization (or your part of it) the most pain; and then to work on the next most painful issue, and so on. It is unethical to ignore painful issues.

The Pain-Directed Ethic attempts to eliminate escape and avoidance from the management style of self and organization. It asks us to identify what is not working both in our own lives and in our organization (or our part of the organization) and then calls on us to address the most severe of these—the issue that represents the greatest threat to our ability or our organization's ability to accomplish our/its purpose. And when that issue or problem is resolved, or when all that can be done today has been done, to move to the next most severe problem, and so on. In this way, the entity in question, whether self or organization, is brought with maximum speed to a more smoothly functioning, integrated whole, and kept there.

When Gandhi said, "Do what is right, now!" it was this ethic (or some version of it) that he must have had in mind. And it was this ethic that the Taoist philosopher, Lao Tsu, must have had in mind when he wrote: "Because the sage always confronts difficulties, he never experiences them"[10] (i.e., he addresses them as soon as they are detected, when they are hardly difficulties at all).

The Pain-Directed Ethic tests the courage, commitment, and creativity of those who would practice it, but it also strengthens those characteristics, and this is important since it is on these characteristics that organizational (and personal) development depends.

> ## Re-statement of Ethic 6
>
> *It is ethical in ongoing personal and organizational development to work first on the issue causing the most pain, and then to work on the next most painful issue, and so on, in this way creating improvements in the sequence most likely to ensure not only survival but also health and wellbeing.* It is unethical to ignore painful issues. By ignoring painful issues, we allow them to compound, threatening all the more the ability of the person or organization to accomplish his or its purpose.

109) What is the issue that is causing you in your part of the organization the most pain (or trouble); the issue that represents a threat to the optimal functioning of you or your organization and about which it is your responsibility to do something. To put it another way, what is the major concern you have regarding your organization (or your division or team)? It may be a personnel issue, a relationship issue, a problem with existing procedures, programs, or products. What is it in your case?

_____
_____
_____

110) Why is this a problem?

_____
_____

111) What anxieties, fears, or concerns, if any, do you have about addressing the issue you've identified?

_____
_____
_____

112) What is the first step in resolving this issue (or, if you already are involved in resolving it, the next step in resolving it)?

_____
_____

113) If you are ready to deal with this problem, when do you plan to take this step (or if you already are dealing with it, when do you plan to take the next step)?

_____

114) By when do you hope to have this problem resolved?

_____

115) What are the implications or consequences of ignoring issues that are causing pain and difficulty within the organization?

    Implications for person who does this?

_____

_____

_____

    Implications for the organization?

_____

_____

_____

116) How would you rate yourself on this ethic? Do you face painful/difficult organizational issues as soon as they present themselves or do you delay? Rate your own performance as it relates to this ethic.

    Excellent ___ Good ___ Average ___ Poor ___

117) If you are not satisfied with your performance on this ethic, what is required in order for you to improve it?

_____

_____

_____

_____

Ethic 7 - The Free Choice Ethic[11]

It is ethical to assume that you are choosing to do all that you do, that you come to your tasks by choice, that you are involved voluntarily.

It is unethical to assume, unless extreme circumstances prevail, that you are being made or forced to do anything.

Ethic 7 presumes that we are choosing our way forward, that no one is making us do anything (unless extreme circumstance prevail), that we are voluntarily involved with the requirements of the organization and of our lives. To presume otherwise is to dis-empower ourselves, and leads to the "victim" mentality.

The victim mentality is disastrous for both the individual who adopts it and for the organization of which he or she is a part. It leads to self-recrimination and the indicting of others. Blame and the denial of responsibility are its hallmarks.

The denial of choice (and of the personal responsibility it implies) is what the French philosopher, Jean Paul Sartre, called "Bad Faith"-- *"pretending things are mandatory when they are in fact voluntary."*[12] Pretending things are mandatory merely represents the extent to which we sometimes are willing to go in order to avoid the hard choices that confront us. Better to confront those choices, Sartre argued, than to presume we have no choice; better to leave the organization, for example, and create a new situation for ourselves than to pretend we are being forced to stay.

Which team faces the greater obstacle, the team comprised of members who believe they are being made to participate, or the team comprised of volunteers?

It is to your advantage and to the advantage of your organization to assume that you are freely choosing to do all that you do within the context of your organization; that you are not being made or forced to do anything. Such an assumption is empowering and eliminates an important impediment to creative and responsible problem-solving.

> **Re-statement of Ethic 7**
>
> *It is ethical to assume that you are freely choosing to do all that you do within the context of your organization, that you come to every task by choice having concluded for yourself that the task is consistent with your values and in service to the organization's mission.* It is unethical to assume that within the context of the organization—the organization you have chosen to join and from which you are free to exit—that you are being made or forced to do anything.

118) How would you rate the members of your organization on this ethic? To what extent are they choosing to be there, choosing to do their jobs, not pretending that they are being forced or made to work? (Rate overall impression.)

    Completely ___ Considerably ___ Somewhat ___ Not at all ___

119) In the course of a week's time, how much resentment do you hear expressed on the part of organizational members, resentment directed toward or concerning other members, supervisors, the tasks that must be performed, the organization as a whole, etc.?

    A Great Deal ___ Considerable ___ Some ___ Hardly any ___

120) How would you rate yourself on this ethic? To what extent are you choosing to fulfill your role in the organization as opposed to feeling that you are being made or forced to do your job?

    Completely ___ Considerably ___ Somewhat ___ Not at all ___

121) Of the organizational tasks that are yours to perform, is there one that you resent doing? If so, what is it?

_____

_____

122) Why do you resent doing it? Is it inconsistent with the organization's mission? Does it violate your values?

_____

_____

_____

123) What are the implications or consequences of pretending you have no choice, of behaving as if you have to do what you are doing?

> (To be clear: There are, of course, victims in this world. Ethic 7 simply encourages us to examine our own role, if any, in creating the "victimhood" we believe we experience. The will of others and forces beyond our control have their say. And at any given moment, these other factors can affect our lives dramatically; affect for example the organizations and relationships of which we are a part, even whether our involvement is possible. But if it is possible, then the Free Choice Ethic offers a cautionary note—and a hopeful one, as well. It states that with respect to the organizations and relationships of which we are a part, we are involved by choice. No one is forcing us to be involved. We are choosing to be involved or choosing not to be involved. And by our choices, our decision-making and follow-through, we participate in the creation of our experience. Yes, there are many factors at play, from the personal to the societal, but the Free Choice Ethic insists that we impose a high standard on ourselves: We have choice, and to an extent greater than we sometimes acknowledge, we craft and compose our lives.)

So, what are the implications or consequences of embracing the victim paradigm, of concluding that you are being forced to do what you are doing at work (even, perhaps, in everyday life)?

Implications for the person who operates in this way?

_____

_____

Implications for co-workers?

_____

_____

Implications for the organization in which this occurs?

_____

_____

Go to the *One Week Action Plan* located at the end of the workbook (p. 81-82).
Answer the Pain-Directed Ethic and the Free Choice Ethic questions.

Ethic 8 - The Conscious Mistakes Ethic

It is ethical to eliminate conscious mistakes. It is unethical to engage in them.

To know that what you are about to do is wrong and to do it anyway is to engage in a conscious mistake. Conscious mistakes are self-destructive. Eventually, they threaten the performance of the individual who engages in them and, in turn, the organization of which the individual is apart.

Mistakes occur and can be useful. We learn from our mistakes. But one of the things we should learn is not to make the same mistake again. "Don't let the same dog bite you twice," is the way songwriter Chuck Berry put it.

To continue to make the same mistake is unethical. It can lead to a life governed by destructive habits, and in some cases, it can lead to addiction. The individual and/or organization with destructive habits, certainly if addiction is involved, is less open, less dynamic, less creative, less able to survive and grow. It is unethical not to reduce and if possible, eliminate conscious mistakes.

> *"This is what ordinary people mean when they say that, although men may differ as to what things are right or wrong, no one ever thinks that it is right to do wrong or wrong to do right."[13]*
> Wilbur Marshall Urban

> # Re-statement of Ethic 8
>
> *It is ethical to reduce and eliminate conscious mistakes.* It is unethical to know that what you are about to do is wrong and to do it anyway.

124) Reflect on your experience in your organization. What are, if any, the conscious mistakes you have made, perhaps even make regularly, in your organization? Look at the rules, policies, your own standards, the standards of the organization. Can you find where you have made or are making conscious mistakes? (If you wish to expand your inquiry, look at your life as a whole and list the conscious mistakes you have made and perhaps continue to make.) Remember, this workbook is for your eyes only.

_____
_____
_____
_____

125) For one or two that you have listed (presuming there are at least one or two), state why you allow (or continue to allow) yourself to do what you know is a mistake. (This is very important. Take your time. You are trying to bring your rationalizations to light for examination and review.)

_____
_____
_____
_____

126) Of the reasons you have given yourself as justification for engaging in conscious mistakes, are there any that strike you as sufficient, i.e., that justify a decision to continue to engage in a particular mistake? Or to put it another way, would it be all right with you if your child used this same rationale to justify engaging in the same conscious mistake?

Yes ___ No ___

127) What are the possible implications or consequences of engaging in work-related conscious mistakes?

    Implications for the person who does this?

_____
_____
_____
_____

    Implications for his or her co-workers? Implications for supervisor?

_____
_____
_____
_____

    Implications for the organization as a whole?

_____
_____
_____
_____

* <u>A Worthwhile Exercise</u>: For the period of one week, count the number of times each day that you engage in a conscious mistake and plot that number at the end of the day on a graph. (You may limit this to conscious mistakes at and with respect to your organization, or you may extend it to the full day.) This can be an illuminating exercise, introducing you to the ways in which you allow conscious mistakes to populate your everyday life and, perhaps, undercut your aims.

Ethic 9 - The Sustainability Ethic

It is ethical to consider the long-range implications of your decision-making and to make sustainability a guiding tenet. It is unethical to knowingly implement practices that ensure the collapse (or diminished health) of the self, the organization, or the environment.

Certain Native American cultures required of their tribal councils that they make decisions with seven generations in mind, the three before theirs and the three after. In this way, they reasoned, the benefits of their way of life would be preserved and available to their descendants.

What these cultures understood was that short term and/or narrow vision leads to practices that can threaten a valued way of life. If, when driving, you look no more than twenty feet in front of you, then you will end up in one traffic jam after another. The chess master plays several moves ahead or is soon checkmated. Similarly, organizations (and individuals) must play "several moves ahead" or they, too, will fail in their effort to accomplish their purpose.

An "organizational trap" is a decision-making practice that trades short-term convenience or gain for long-term inconvenience or loss.[14] It may be inconvenient to go "the extra mile" with a customer, you may not be in the mood for it, but to "brush off" or "sell short" a customer is to walk your organization into a trap. The long-term consequence is not only the loss of business but the loss of reputation, as well.

With every decision, and with all existing organizational practices, the question to ask is this: *Will this decision (if made) or this organizational practice (if continued) allow the organization to sustain itself, and move ever more surely in the direction of its completed mission? Or will it make for a future in which it will be harder for the organization to accomplish its purpose?* The ethical course requires sustainability. It leads toward a future—the unforeseen aside—increasingly supportive of both individual and organizational development.

It is this ethic that addresses the health and viability of the physical and biological environment. If organizations—through their practices—destroy the environment, *choosing short-term gain over sustainability,* then they destroy themselves.[15]

> *"The industrial nations have come far enough down the road to affluence to recognize that more goods do not necessarily mean more happiness. They are also recognizing that more goods eventually mean more junk, and that the junk in the air, in the water and on the land could make the earth unfit for human habitation . . . "*[16]

Henry Ford II

> # Re-statement of Ethic 9
>
> *It is ethical to submit all personal, organizational, cultural, and environmental practices to close scrutiny, altering them until they are as sustainable and free of traps, as possible.* It is unethical to knowingly implement practices that ensure environmental collapse, and unethical, as well, to implement practices that diminish the health and wellbeing of individuals.

128) How would you rate your organization on this ethic, on the extent to which sustainability is a guiding tenet in its decision-making overall?

       Excellent ___ Good ___ Average ___ Poor ___

129) In your opinion, are there currently at your organization practices that threaten the long-term survival and success of your organization and/or practices that threaten the long-term wellbeing of the broader environment in which your organization will have to function?

       Yes ___ No ___

130) If yes, what are they?

_____

_____

_____

131) Do you have an idea or suggestion for changing one or more of these practices, an idea that would allow your organization to meet current needs with practices consistent with long term survival and success?

       Yes ___ No ___

132) Have you shared your suggestion (or proposed solution) with others who might be able to assess it and if in agreement, assist with its implementation? If not, why not?

_____

_____

_____

133) How would you rate yourself on this ethic? With respect to the areas of the organization for which you have responsibility, how good a job have you done of making sustainability a guiding tenet in your decision-making?

Excellent ___   Good ___   Average ___   Poor ___

134) Is there an area for which you have responsibility that currently is governed by short-term considerations at the expense of long-term organizational success, i.e., a trap? If so, what is it?

_____

_____

_____

135) What do you propose to do about it? What is your plan for getting your part of the organization out of this "trap?"

_____

_____

_____

136) Overall, how would you rate your organization in the following areas, each of which has important long-term implications for the organization:

Scale: 4 = Excellent   3 = Good   2 = Average   1 = Poor

Rating:

Accounting Practices _____
Accountability (Checks & Balances) _____
Advertising Practices _____
Community Relations _____
Energy-Efficiency _____
Environmentally-safe products _____
Environmentally-safe production _____
Hiring Practices _____
Management/Leadership Practices _____
Promotion and Advancement Practices _____
Re-cycling of materials _____
Teamwork _____
Training _____

137) Which of these is most in need of improvement?

_____

Ethic 10 - The Wind Harp Ethic

It is ethical to treat others in and out of the organization as you would like to be treated even though you are not always so treated. It is unethical not to find appropriate avenues for the release of your anger, resentment, and rage. It is unethical to engage in scapegoating.

Legend has it that during the Middle Ages there existed an instrument called the Wind Harp. The wind harp could be positioned in the window of a mud and straw hut in such a way that wind entering the instrument from one side exited the other side as music. "We are all wind harps," declared the Romantic Poets[17] or could choose to be. The idea being that it might be possible to control ourselves to such an extent that no matter the "ill-wind", we do not take out our anger, resentment, or rage on others.

Put two monkeys in a cage and shock one and the shocked monkey will begin biting, hitting, and scratching the innocent by-standing monkey. This is not unlike what happens in organizations when, for example, a supervisor treats rudely his supervisees because he (or she) was treated rudely by his supervisor.

Gandhi said, "Be the change you expect," and with that statement captured the requirement of the Wind Harp Ethic, especially if you believe you are worthy of courtesy, fair treatment, and respect. The Wind Harp Ethic requires that you extend courtesy, fairness, and respect to others even if you do not always receive such treatment yourself.

It is this ethic that would have you treat others (regardless of age, gender, race, culture, etc.) as you would have your mother/sister/daughter and/or father/brother/son treated. By this ethic we are led to the openness and sensitivity that unity in diversity requires. [18]

The Wind Harp Ethic profits both the individual who practices it and the organization of which he or she is a part by stopping before it starts the damaging impact of careless and negative interpersonal treatment.

> ## Re-statement of Ethic 10
>
> *It is ethical to treat others in and out of the organization as you would like to be treated even though you are not always so treated.* It is unethical not to find appropriate avenues for the release of your anger, resentment and rage so as to keep from passing them on to or taking them out on others. It is unethical to engage in scapegoating.

138) How would you rate your organization on this ethic? How would you rate the caliber of interpersonal treatment exchanged between organizational members and between organizational members and those impacted by the organization (i.e., consumers, customers, organizational neighbors, others using the same space & resources)?

        Excellent ___ Good ___ Average ___ Poor ___

139) In your opinion, are there individual *members of the organization* who happen to belong to a given group who are treated inappropriately **simply because they are members of that group?**

        Yes ___ No ___

140) If there are individuals within the organization who are mistreated simply because they belong to a particular group, in what way are they mistreated?

_____
_____
_____

141) In what way can this situation be corrected so that the organization can avoid the trap inherent in such mistreatment?

_____
_____
_____
_____
_____
_____

142) In your opinion, are there individuals *outside the organization, individuals who are impacted by the organization*, who are treated inappropriately **simply because they belong to a particular group?**

Yes ___ No ___

143) If there are individuals outside the organization who are mistreated simply because they belong to a particular group, in what way are they mistreated?

_____
_____
_____

144) In what way can this situation be corrected so that the organization can avoid the trap inherent in such mistreatment?

_____
_____
_____

145) How would you rate yourself on this ethic? How good are you at treating others like you would like to be treated whether in the organization or impacted by it (its customers, neighbors, etc.)?

Excellent ___ Good ___ Average ___ Poor ___

146) If there are individuals you find it difficult to work with or serve (whether they be inside the organization or out), are you able to move beyond that difficulty and treat them like you would like to be treated? To put it another way, are you able to ignore the feelings that arise in you in their presence *and continue with valued behavior,* behavior called for by this ethic?

Yes ___ No ___

147) If not, *and if you are willing*, what might you do in order to make it possible for you to treat them properly?

_____
_____
_____

148) How would you rate yourself on your ability to not treat others rudely or abusively even though you have been so treated, recently or otherwise? How good are you at not taking out on others your anger, resentment, irritability, bad mood, rage, etc.?

Excellent ___ Good ___ Average ___ Poor ___

149) To what extent do you find that you carry anger, resentment, and/or rage inside of you?

A lot ___ Somewhat ___ Not at all ___

150) Have you found appropriate avenues for the release of these feelings so that you are not releasing them (taking them out) on others or on yourself? *(Note: It is important for your own wellbeing as well as for the wellbeing of others that you find appropriate avenues for the release of your anger, resentment, and rage. Over-eating, drug and alcohol abuse, self-recrimination, depression, addictions of all sorts are ways in which we attempt to live and cope with the anger and rage we hold within us. All are self-destructive. For your own sake as well as for the sake of others, it is important to find creative, constructive, therapeutic releases for these feelings, feelings that are normal, feelings that must be acknowledged and finally, feelings that must be released safely if we are to honor ourselves and those around us.)*

Yes ___ No ___

151) If yes, what are they?

_____
_____
_____
_____
_____

Go to the *One Week Action Plan* (p. 82) and answer the Conscious Mistakes Ethic, the Sustainability Ethic, and the Wind Harp Ethic questions.

This page is reserved for notes and reflections, also for questions and exercises used in *The Ethics of Human Development Workshop.*

Ethic 11 - The Personal Growth Ethic

*It is ethical to continue to grow as a person, to continue to increase your capacity to conduct yourself in accord with your ethics and principles.
It is unethical to stop growing as a person.*

The growth of the organization depends upon the personal growth of its members. For that reason, individuals profit not only themselves but also their organization when they increase their capacity to live in accord with their ethics and principles.

The Personal Growth Ethic calls on us to increase our capacity to conduct ourselves in accord with our ethics and principles. It makes personal growth a requirement, inviting us to identify what we must work on next to grow as persons.

With respect to this task (the task of identifying what to work on next), the work of Ken Keyes, a student of human potential, is pertinent. Keyes wrote that there are two kinds of people in the world, *lovers and teachers.* Lovers are those people who—through their interactions with us—introduce us to those behaviors, qualities, traits, attitudes in us that we love. Teachers, on the other hand, are those people who—through their interactions with us—introduce us to those behaviors, qualities, traits, attitudes in us that we do not love. And there are no other kinds of people in the world.[19]

Adopting the "lovers'/teachers'" perspective allows us to identify what you must work on next to grow as a person. When an interaction with a "teacher" occurs, an interaction that causes you anxiety or discomfort or that makes you feel ineffective, you are invited to look carefully at yourself and to identify the desirable attitude or skill which, if acquired, would allow you to be more relaxed, more effective should the situation occur again. In this way, the lovers'/teachers' perspective helps us identify our personal growth curriculum.

It is vital that we learn from our "teachers." We may abhor their teaching method but, at base, they are doing us a favor since they are inviting us to learn, let's say, *patience, courage, forgiveness, compassion,* any number of desirable ways of being with others. And by learning and growing in this way we strengthen and make more vital not only ourselves but our organizations.[20] It was to this process of personal growth that the economist E. F. Schumacher referred when he wrote that "work exists for the refinement of character."

> # Re-statement of Ethic 11
>
> *It is ethical to continue to grow as a person, to continue to increase your capacity to conduct yourself in accord with your ethics and principles.* It is unethical not to continue the life-long process of personal development.

152) How would you rate yourself on this ethic, on your willingness to do what you know must be done if you are to grow as a person?

      Excellent ___ Good ___ Average ___ Poor ___

153) Think about the "teachers" in your life. In your judgment, what are the desirable skills, behaviors, or traits they are trying to teach you, the skills, behaviors, or traits which, if acquired, will allow you to be yourself around them and/or deal more effectively with them.

_____
_____
_____

154) Which skill, behavior, or trait of those you are being invited to learn by your "teachers" do you feel is the most important one for you to learn first?

_____
_____

155) How do you plan to go about learning it? What is your first or next step?

_____
_____
_____

156) "Openness" and "willingness" are keys to individual development. Without them, development is slowed. How open would you say you are to listening to new ideas, or trying new ways of doing things? Do you seek out new experiences for yourself or are you inclined to let them come to you? If "100" reflects a total openness to life (not fool-hearty or reckless but thoughtful and self-respecting) and "0" represents little openness at all to what is new or different, what score would you give yourself?

_____

157) What about your commitment to personal growth, to the task of increasing your capacity to behave in accord with your ethics and principles? If "100" reflects a total commitment to personal growth and "0" represents little or no commitment to personal growth, what score would you give yourself? (Before you answer, think about what you have done that reflects your level of commitment. This question is about what your actions in recent weeks, months, and years indicate is your commitment to growing as a person.)

_____

158) What are the benefits associated with this ethic?

Benefits for the person who pursues the requirements of this ethic?

_____
_____
_____
_____
_____

Benefits/implications for an organization comprised largely of individuals who pursue the requirements of this ethic?

_____
_____
_____
_____
_____

Ethic 12 - The Gift-Sharing Ethic

It is ethical to utilize your gifts, talents, and unique experience on behalf of your organization. It is unethical not to share your gifts, talents, and unique experience somewhere, for the benefit of someone.

Buckminster Fuller, inventor, poet and philosopher, said: "You can assume that you are fulfilling your purpose if you are in the process of turning your experience into products and events that bring advantage to others."[21]

Your organization is one place to share your gifts and talents. It is helpful to do so because by sharing them you (likely) strengthen the organization, increasing its versatility and capacity to adapt. But it also is important for the quality of your everyday work experience. To the extent that you turn your gifts, talents, and unique knowledge and experience to the benefit of your organization, and through your organization to the benefit of others, then to that extent you will feel a well-earned sense of satisfaction. You will feel yourself in the process of fulfilling your purpose and this invariably enhances the quality of life.

It should be added, however, that you may not be able to share your gifts and unique knowledge with your organization. Your organization may not need or want them. That is possible. However, *it must be emphasized that it is unethical not to share your gifts, talents, and unique knowledge and experience somewhere, for the benefit of someone.*[23] The organization you have chosen to join, whose mission and values you accept, is an excellent place to share them but it is not the only place to share them. The task is to find some way to serve and perhaps enrich others—and yourself—through the sharing of what is uniquely you.

> # Re-statement of Ethic 12
>
> *It is ethical to utilize your gifts, talents, and unique experience on behalf of your organization. Through the expression of your unique gifts, you may help your organization evolve and in the process acquire for yourself a greater sense of purpose and meaning.* It is unethical not to share your gifts, talents, and unique experience somewhere, for the benefit of someone; and your organization does represent one place, if not the only place, where sharing your gifts benefits others.

159) In what way are you turning your gifts, talents, and/or unique experience and knowledge to the benefit of others? Think about it. In what way are you making a difference for others? Don't be shy or overly modest. Your knowledge or experience is making a difference for someone (maybe many people), perhaps your children, your students, fellow employees, friends, a neighbor. Take a moment and list the way (or ways) in which you are making a difference for others.

_____
_____
_____

160) Imagine that at the bottom of your current job description, the following was added:

> *'And lastly, the individual holding this position should re-create it, he/she should make it new. The new version should include all that the organization found useful in the previous version while adding that which for the first time now is possible given the unique talents of the new job holder.'*
>
> *'The process of re-creating this position should be done so carefully that the workplace never (or only very briefly) experiences the slightest decrement in overall performance.'*

This addition to one's job description brings the requirements of this ethic to the workplace. The presumption, it should be remembered, is that the "re-creation of one's position" serves not only the organization but one's own job satisfaction, as well.

So, in the space provided at the top of the next page, consider what you might do in your current work were you to take this change to your job description seriously.

_____
_____
_____
_____
_____
_____

161) Why is it important that you share your gifts, talents, unique knowledge and experience with others? **To put it more exactly, why is it important that you draw on your gifts, talents, and knowledge—what is uniquely you—to create helpful, enjoyable, meaningful, or enriching experiences for others?** (We're not talking about imposing yourself where what you have to offer is not wanted. We're talking about figuring out a way to share what is uniquely you where it might make a difference for others.)

Why is it important that you do this? What do you get out of it?

_____
_____
_____

What might others get out of it?

_____
_____
_____

How could an organization benefit if this was a common practice within it, individuals looking for ways to share the best of who they are and what they know?

_____
_____
_____
_____
_____

162) There is an African proverb that states: ***"when the lives of the world are thrown into the air, everyone reaches for their own."*** What this suggests is that at a deep and fundamental level, we love ourselves. It's not that we can't be disappointed with ourselves, go through long periods of self-dislike, depression, or despair; that is possible and does happen. But beyond that, if we quiet ourselves and think about it, we usually see that we care deeply about the life we have been given, so much so that if the lives of the world were thrown into the air, we would reach for our own.

On the lines provided below, indicate why you are grateful that you are who you are. Gratefulness is a state of being from which it is easier and more natural to behave toward others with generosity and true concern. Remembering how grateful we are to have the life we have been given opens us to the sharing of ourselves in ways more likely to benefit others.

If the lives of the world were thrown into the air, why would you reach for your own?

_____
_____
_____
_____
_____
_____
_____
_____
_____

Go to the *One Week Action Plan* (p. 83) and answer the Personal Growth Ethic and the Gift-Sharing Ethic questions.

Conclusion

If you are reading this after having completed the workbook, then congratulations are in order. You have just put yourself and your organization through a rigorous examination. While not always a comfortable thing to do, it nevertheless is an extremely worthwhile thing to do. From this process you gain clarity. By telling yourself the truth about your relationship to your organization, you have set an ethical course, one likely to bring advantage both to you and to your organization.

The next step is to proceed with your ethical conduct objectives. That is what the *One Week Action Plan* is about. Turn to it and select one or two objectives that you will undertake and perhaps complete in the coming week. Select the one or two that you feel confident about completing. And once selected, complete it if you can.

As you proceed, you will be doing two things at once. You will be exercising your capacity to act in accord with your principles, your capacity to ethically and creatively resolve an issue that needs your attention. And you will be serving your organization, perhaps by "fixing" a problem, perhaps simply by making available to your organization a person (you) now more fully engaged and capable.

Notes

[1] I want to acknowledge the work of certain writers whose work has influenced me greatly; in particular, John David Garcia and R. Buckminster Fuller. Garcia's books, *The Moral Society* and *Creative Transformation*, impressed me deeply with their power and clarity. His identification of the ethics required for creative and evolutionary advance along with his analysis of the relationship of ethics to bureaucracy are brilliant accomplishments to which this document owes much.

Fuller is one of the intellectual giants of the Twentieth Century. It was Fuller who, after fifty years of careful study, concluded that humanity's future depends not on scientific discovery or on governmental or religious structure but rather, and above all, on the integrity of each individual. When he wrote about ethics, as he did in *Critical Path*, he did so with great insight and precision.

Ethics defined: "the study of standards of conduct"--Webster's New World Dictionary, Second Edition; to the question, *"How ought I to behave?"* the philosopher Immanuel Kant wrote, *"Ethics provides the answer."*

NOTE: No matter how complete and thorough the recommended code of conduct (for example, the ethics of human development), there will be moments that call for totally unique responses, responses different and more "ethical" than those prescribed by the code. When that happens, your obligation is to the moment and not to the code. *"Be it how it will, do right now,"* is the way Emerson put it, even if it means abandoning the code. The expert chef follows the recipe to a "T" until knowledge or intuition tells him or her that by varying the recipe, he or she can produce a more perfect dish. There will be exceptions to the ethics of human development but in general—when in doubt—they prescribe the safest direction in which to err.

[2] Garcia, John David, *Creative Transformation: A Practical Guide for Maximizing Creativity*, Noetic Press, Eugene, OR & Whitmore Publishing Company, Inc., Ardmore, PA, 1991, p. 151-153. This ethic comes directly from Garcia's work, combining two of eight ethical principles he proposes for increasing creativity. He argues that *"it is unethical to be certain"* and therefore, *"ethical to doubt"* for the reasons noted in the text. This is also a central theme in Canadian writer, John Ralston Saul's *The Unconscious Civilization*, House of Anansi Press Limited: Concord, Ontario, 1995, p.190. "The examined life makes a virtue of uncertainty. It celebrates doubt."

[3] *Ibid.* p. 152.

[4] *Ibid.* Garcia writes: *"Our models of nature cannot evolve unless we doubt their validity."* p. 140.

[5] *Ibid.* *"Inaction is unethical";* another of Garcia's ethical principles for increasing creativity. p. 153.

[6] *Ibid.* p. 153.

[7] *Ibid.* Garcia writes: *"When we love someone we must give them clear and unavoidable negative feedback when they are destructive, recognizing that they may be right and that we may be in error."* p. 270. This point was made in another way by William Blake with his concept of "double vision," the notion that what we see (hear/feel/say) reveals as much about us and what we value as it does about what is available to be seen (heard/felt/said/etc.).

[8] *Ibid.* p. 142.

[9] Peck, M. Scott, *The Road Less Traveled.* New York: Simon and Schuster, Publishers, 1978, p. 62 – 63.

[10] Lao Tsu, *The Tao Te Ching.* Vintage Books: New York, 1989, p. 65.

[11] Ethic 7 raises a complicated and delicate issue: namely, the presumption of choice. We have and make choices and are free to do so. We are not the victims we sometimes portray ourselves to be.

But is that so: *We make choices and are free to do so?* It is certainly the case that our histories obviously and dramatically affect the choices we make. It might even be accurate to say that our histories determine the choices we make, a statement that undercuts the notion of free choice altogether. We are not outside the web of cause and effect; we are within it, a part of it, everyone acting in accord with the causes that impinge upon them. Where is the freedom in a system in which actions flow necessarily from what has preceded them?

And yet, our histories are learning histories. We learn from our experience. We learn to observe, to engage in forethought, to think about what will happen if we do this or that. We become conscious. And as we become conscious, options appear. At some point, it seems natural and appropriate to say that we have choices. Appropriate, also, to say that we have responsibility for the choices we make.

Is this illusion? Does the complexity of our learning history prevent us from seeing the "determinism" that operates in our lives? Perhaps. In fact, it may not be possible to dispense with that possibility. However, what is presumed here is this: To develop and mature is to experience a shift in the locus of control from past conditioning to a conscious, deliberative, and aware self. This is a gradual shift brought about by the consequences of past acts, consequences that encourage us to pay attention, to think for ourselves, to consider the likely consequences of our future acts. We learn to pause, to reflect, to interrupt what were previously automatic chains of behavior with decisions to proceed or not to proceed. And with those learned skills, we become self-directing. We begin to choose our way forward, and we hold ourselves responsible for the choices we make, insisting that we learn from our mistakes—insisting, as well, that ethic, principle, goal, or vision govern our choices, not the restraints of past conditioning.

There are victims in this world, of course; far, far too many individuals who lack options and/or who did not in any meaningful sense choose or help create the situation in which they find themselves. And there are individuals whose learning histories are so distorted or incomplete that in the face of alternative options, they continue to choose the self-destructive. All of this is true, and true perhaps for all of us to some degree. The point here, however, is that it is possible to learn not to make victims of ourselves, not to make choices that are self-destructive; possible to acquire a learning history that supports the pursuit of personal development and responsible decision-making.

[12] Berger, Peter, *Invitation to Sociology: A Humanistic Perspective.* Doubleday & Co., Inc.: Garden City, New York, 1963, p. 143.

[13] Urban, Wilbur Marshall, *Fundamentals of Ethics.* New York: Henry Holt and Company, Inc., 1939, p. 337.

[14] Platt, John R., "Social Traps." In *American Psychologist,* Vol. 28, #8, August, 1973, pgs. 641-651.

[15] The classic illustration of this phenomenon is "the tragedy of the commons." See Garrett Hardin, "The Tragedy of the Commons," *Science*, Vol. 162, 1968, pg. 1243-1248.

[16] Ford II, Henry, *The Human Environment and Business.* Weybright and Talley, Inc.: New York, 1970, p. 52.

[17] For more on the Wind Harp, see the work of Owen Barfield. *The Rediscovery of Meaning and Other Essays,* Wesleyan University Press: Middletown, Conn., 1977, p. 65-78.

[18] Here I have in mind the full range of "isms" or stereotypes that have us respond to others as though they are categories and not individuals (i.e., age, disability, sexual orientation, etc.).

[19] Keyes, Jr., Ken, *The Handbook of Higher Consciousness.* Loveline Bks: Coos Bay, OR, 1990.

[20] A corollary of this ethic is that it is ethical to seek out professional help, guidance and continuing education in your effort to grow as a person.

[21] Fuller, Buckminster, "The Fifty-Year Experiment," an audio tape published by New Dimensions, San Francisco, CA., 1982.

[22] The Gift Sharing Ethic also is drawn from the work of Garcia. See footnotes 1 and 2.

The One Week Action Plan

Instructions: *List on the lines provided your specific ethical conduct objectives.* **Make sure to state each of them in the form of an "action statement"** *(e.g., "Talk to individual "xx" on Monday about my view of his performance; Enroll in training seminar; Ask "yy" for feedback on my work; Meet with supervisor to develop plan for solving personnel problem; etc.) Then, at the end of one week, indicate whether or not you have "undertaken" and/or "completed" the objectives you have chosen to work on. (Numbers refer to workbook questions.)*

Objectives: Undertaken   Completed

Organizational Ethic (see questions 13 - 15): Is there anything you should do to improve the efficiency with which you work? the accuracy of your work? your everyday demeanor or pleasantness?

_____

_____

_____   _____   _____

Organizational Ethic (see questions 20 - 21): Is there anything you can do for those around you to eliminate unnecessary hardship or distraction?

_____

_____

_____   _____   _____

Organizational Ethic (see questions 57 – 63): Is there a step you must take to improve the fit between you and your job? Or do you need to develop an exit strategy that honors both you and the organization? Is a discussion with anyone required?

_____

_____

_____   _____   _____

Objectives: Undertaken   Completed

Open-Mindedness Ethic (see questions 66-68, 74-75): Is there anything you feel you need to do to increase your "openness" so that creativity—both yours and that of others—is served?

_____

_____

_____   _____   _____

Deliberate Action Ethic (see questions 82 - 84): Is there a job duty or area of responsibility that you have left for too long on "automatic pilot"; an area that would profit from a careful re-thinking? If so, what do you need to do?

_____

_____

_____   _____   _____

Feedback Ethic (see questions 88 - 89): Is there someone or some group from whom you should solicit feedback to ensure that you are truly serving their needs? If so, what do you need to do next?

_____

_____

_____   _____   _____

Feedback Ethic (see question 93): Is there someone or some group to whom you need to express your appreciation? If so, who? When? How?

_____

_____

_____   _____   _____

Objectives: Undertaken   Completed

Feedback Ethic (see question 94): Is there someone or some group whose performance is hurting the organization, someone or some group to whom you need to offer corrective or negative feedback? If so, who? When? How?

_____

_____

_____   _____   _____

Truth-Telling Ethic (see questions 103 - 105): Is there some step that you can imagine taking that would increase your capacity for truth-telling? An issue that must be resolved; a contradiction that must be addressed; a skill that must be acquired?

_____

_____

_____   _____   _____

Pain-Directed Ethic (see question 109 - 114): What do you plan to do about the issue that is causing your part of the organization the most "pain"; and therefore, that weakens to a degree organizational performance?

_____

_____

_____   _____   _____

Pain-Directed Ethic (see questions 116 - 117): What must you do, if anything, to decrease your "response time"; i.e., to respond to painful issues sooner after they arise and therefore, not procrastinate so much? Is there a concrete step you can take?

_____

_____

_____   _____   _____

Objectives: Undertaken   Completed

Free Choice Ethic (see questions 120 - 122): Is there
a step you need to take to eliminate your
resistance to specific duties so that you can do them
without resentment, choosing to do them rather than
pretending you are being forced to do them? What is it?

_____

_____

_____   _____

Conscious Mistakes Ethic (see questions 124 - 126):
What conscious mistakes, if any, do you plan to cut
down on; eliminate? How?

_____

_____

_____   _____   _____

Sustainability Ethic (see questions 133 - 135): Is there
a "trap" in your part of the organization (or overall)
that you propose to do something about? What is the next
step you plan to take?

_____

_____

_____   _____   _____

Wind Harp Ethic (see questions 139 – 144): Is there a
step you think you should take to ensure that your
organization is treating all groups—whether inside the
organization or out—fairly, ethically? What is it?

_____

_____

_____   _____   _____

Objectives: Undertaken Completed

Wind Harp Ethic (see questions 145 - 151): If there are individuals you find it difficult to work with or serve (whether they are inside the organization or out), what is the next thing you need to do to move beyond that difficulty and treat them like you would like to be treated? What do you need to do to ignore the feelings that arise in you in their presence and *continue with valued behavior?*

_____

_____

_____   _____ _____

Personal Growth Ethic (see questions 153 - 155): What is the next step you plan to take in acquiring the skill, trait, or behavior that you are being invited to learn by your "teacher(s)"?

_____

_____

_____   _____ _____

Gift-Sharing Ethic (see question 160): Is there some important way that you are not being used by your organization or workplace, some way that would utilize your gifts/skills/knowledge more fully and more effectively? If so, what step might you take to explore this possibility?

_____

_____

_____   _____ _____

Other Ethics of Human Development books:

The Ethics of Human Development Quick Guide

A small handbook (32 pages) providing the reader with ready access to the ethics of human development and their corollaries. Also included are quotes from a variety of sources suggesting the meaning of each ethic.

The Ethics of Human Development Training Program – A Complete Guide

The Ethics of Human Development Training Program is detailed in this book. The ethics of human development are defined and tools for teaching the ethics (role-playing scripts, extensive rationales, etc.) are provided. For individuals, teachers, trainers and human resource personnel interested in providing ethics of human development training in their organizations and classrooms.

Right Livelihood: The Twelve Ethics of Work

A young man, perhaps in his early 20s, visits his uncle who discusses with him the ethics of work, ethics based on human logic.

This book is ideal for high school and college students, also for individuals just entering the workforce, individuals interested in a work ethic consistent with a *right livelihood*.

Human Logic and the Theater of Everyday Life

Human Logic and the Theater of Everyday Life is about the journey of the individual through the ups and down of everyday life, the journey we take to whatever maturity and enlightenment is ours to obtain.

The aim of the book: to aid us in our effort to act wisely in the theater of everyday life, while also helping us evolve the many organizations of which we are a part.

The above books can be ordered through area booksellers.

To contact Dr. Thomas --
Email: dtec@cox.net
Website: davidthomasphd.com

www.ingramcontent.com/pod-product-compliance
Lightning Source LLC
Chambersburg PA
CBHW051214290426
44109CB00021B/2450